D0116063

J307.76   Shapley, Robert W.
SHA

       Boomtowns

Valley of the Tetons
Public Library
Victor, Idaho

The Wild West in American History

BOOMTOWNS

Written by Robert W. Shapley
Illustrated by Luciano Lazzarino
Edited by Arlene C. Rourke

© 1990 by Rourke Publications, Inc.

All rights reserved. No part of this book may be reproduced or
utilized in any form or by any means, electronic or mechanical
including photocopying, recording, or by any information
storage and retrieval system without permission in writing
from the publisher.

Library of Congress Cataloging-in-Publication Data

Shapley, Robert W., 1927-
   Boomtowns / by Robert W. Shapley.
      p.   cm. —(The Wild West in American history)
   1. Cities and towns—West (U.S.)—History—19th century—
Juvenile literature. 2. Cities and towns—West (U.S.)—Growth—
History—19th century—Juvenile literature. 3. West (U.S.)—Social
conditions. 4. Frontier and pioneer life—West (U.S.)—History—
19th century—Juvenile literature. I. Title. II. Series.
HT123.5.A17S54 1990
307.76'0978'09034—dc20   89-6152
                                                                                CIP
   ISBN 0-86625-370-X   AC

Rourke Publications, Inc.
Vero Beach, Florida 32964

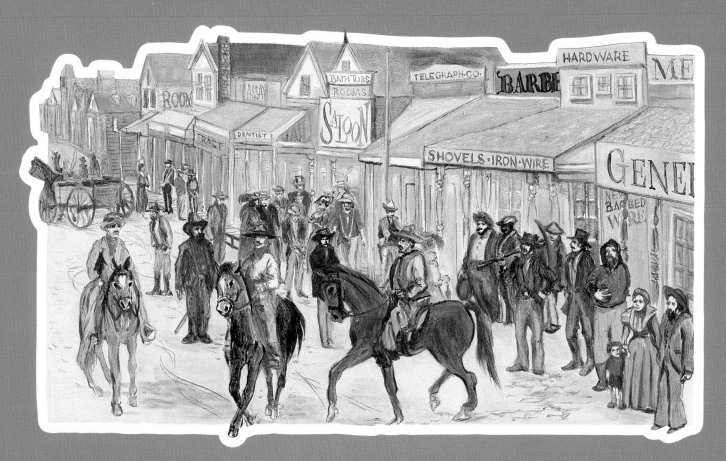

BOOMTOWNS

In the early 1800s, few people had traveled into the wild, dangerous land west of the Mississippi River. Millions of shaggy buffalo roamed there on grassy plains that stretched hundreds of miles to the Rocky Mountains. Indian tribes lived on the land as their ancestors had done since time immemorial.

Then, in 1849, something happened that brought great changes to the West. In the Territory of California, a worker at a frontier sawmill found some tiny grains of a yellow metal in a stream.

News of that gold find spread like a wildfire. Within a short time, thousands of men were heading west with hopes of finding gold and getting rich.

Hundreds of miners rushed to each rugged mountain area where gold was found. In a short time, traders arrived with wagonloads of merchandise and supplies. A small town would start to grow. Some of these towns sprang up almost overnight. These fast-growing areas came to be known as "boomtowns."

The thirst for gold was not the only reason for the rise of boomtowns. These were the years of the "long drive." Texas cowboys spent weeks on the open ranges driving large cattle herds north for hundreds of miles. When the long drives were over, the cowboys would let off steam in the boomtowns before starting on the long trip back home to Texas.

All boomtowns were lively places, filled with loud music, excitement, and adventure. They were places where cowpokes could trade tales about the dangers found on the frontier. These boomtowns, and the people who were a part of them, played a special role in the growth of our nation.

THE GOLD RUSH

When cries of "Gold! They found gold in California!" rang through the streets in eastern cities and towns, people went wild. Lust for gold drove many men west. These men were called "49ers" because the gold rush started in the year 1849. A few 49ers made fortunes beyond their wildest dreams. Some found just enough gold to get by. Most found little or no gold.

In their wild search for gold, the 49ers faced danger and death from wild animals, deserts, disease, Indian attacks, and gunfighters. Miners lived in miserable conditions in mining camps and later in boomtowns.

After all the gold in one area had been mined, miners moved on to better digs elsewhere. Behind them they left empty camps and sometimes empty towns. These towns were called "ghost towns." Buildings in these deserted towns decayed and fell into disrepair. Weeds and bushes grew in the once crowded streets as the wilderness again reclaimed the land.

On the other hand, many boomtowns grew and prospered. Today, some are important business centers. A few have been restored so that visitors can wander through the old buildings to see a real western boomtown firsthand.

The boomtown era started in the mid 1800s and lasted only about four decades. Boomtowns had many similarities. It was the people and events connected with a boomtown that made each one unique.

Major mining regions for gold, silver, lead, and copper.

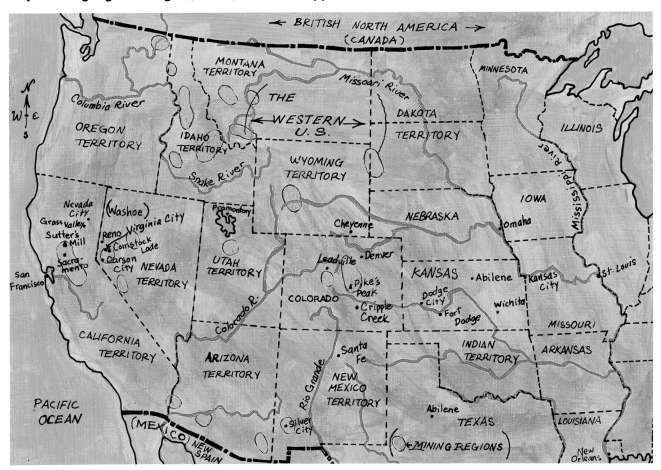

The harbor and streets of San Francisco bustled with people with one thing on their minds—gold!

THE FIRST BOOMTOWN

Just before the first big gold strike was made, San Francisco was a small harbor in a bay on the Pacific Ocean. The harbor was in the Territory of California and had a population of about 800 people. In the year 1848, a sawmill worker named James Marshall found gold near a frontier trading post called Sutter's Mill. The post was located in the mountains far to the northeast of the harbor. The events that followed that gold strike turned San Francisco into one of the biggest, busiest boomtowns in western history.

When news of the gold strike reached the eastern states, thousands of men headed for California. One way of getting there was on sailing ships. The long ocean trip took months because the ships had to sail far south around the tip of South America. Hundreds of ships made the dangerous trip, carrying men who were eager to get to the gold fields. These ships also carried supplies to sustain them when they got there.

Day after day, ships arrived at the small port of San Francisco. Future miners hurried ashore, glad to be on land after many months at sea. Harbor workers unloaded tons of supplies carried in the holds.

In a short time, the tiny port mushroomed into a noisy, bustling boomtown. Americans weren't the only people lured to California by gold. News of the gold strike spread worldwide. The new boomtown filled with men from such faraway places as England, France, Germany, and South America. All of these people needed to be outfitted with equipment and supplies before heading for the gold fields located many miles inland.

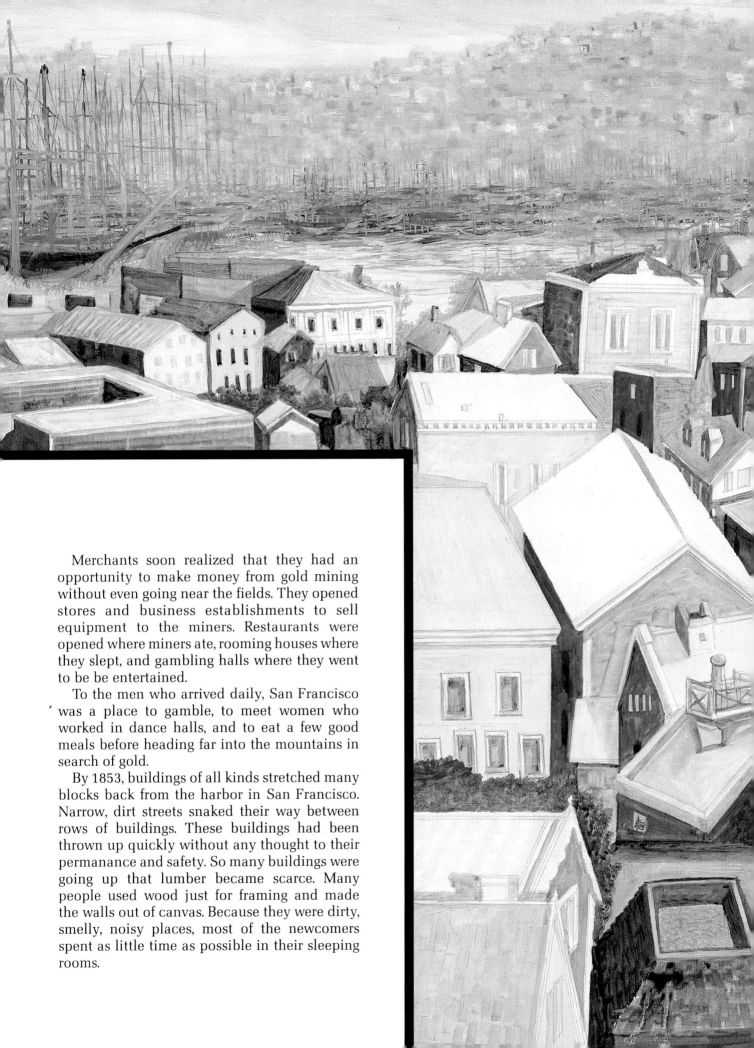

Merchants soon realized that they had an opportunity to make money from gold mining without even going near the fields. They opened stores and business establishments to sell equipment to the miners. Restaurants were opened where miners ate, rooming houses where they slept, and gambling halls where they went to be be entertained.

To the men who arrived daily, San Francisco was a place to gamble, to meet women who worked in dance halls, and to eat a few good meals before heading far into the mountains in search of gold.

By 1853, buildings of all kinds stretched many blocks back from the harbor in San Francisco. Narrow, dirt streets snaked their way between rows of buildings. These buildings had been thrown up quickly without any thought to their permanance and safety. So many buildings were going up that lumber became scarce. Many people used wood just for framing and made the walls out of canvas. Because they were dirty, smelly, noisy places, most of the newcomers spent as little time as possible in their sleeping rooms.

During the height of the gold rush in the early 1850s, the boomtowners could boast that San Francisco had nearly 500 saloons, 150 eating places, and 50 gambling halls.

By the year 1852, miners who had struck gold were returning to San Francisco. They boasted of their luck and looked for some fun in the booming seaport before going back to the hard life in the gold fields. Some say that San Francisco existed only to get money from miners. Some foolhardy 49ers acted as if they didn't care what happened to them or their money as long as they could enjoy themselves. Many of the men were oblivious to the hidden dangers of a large boomtown. Dark streets and unlighted hallways provided perfect places for robbers. Many a miner was relieved of his hard won gold in just this way.

Danger came not only from robbers. It also came in the form of fire. The rickety, wooden buildings, sitting side by side were fire traps. During its early years, the booming San Francisco experienced several serious fires. Flames and sparks leaped from building to building and burned down large sections of the town. Wood stoves and kerosene lamps started many of the fires. Law officers of the times blamed some of these fires on gangs. Lawless groups of men would start a fire in one block as a distraction. While people rushed to fight the fires or to watch them burn, the gang would go to other areas to rob and loot buildings.

In spite of these problems, people who had businesses in the boomtown made thousands of dollars off the gold rush. After working hard they wanted to live well. Soon finer buildings started to appear. Other signs of good times showed up in the form of newspapers, hospitals, and churches. However, even with growth, the rowdiness and dangers of the boomtown were still present. In 1854 and 1855, a serious crime wave occurred. Officials and local townspeople got together to bring law and order to the booming area. The citizens who wanted to fight the criminals formed into groups called "vigilantes." They helped catch and hang several murderers and they aided in driving hundreds of other lawbreakers out of town.

The first year after the gold fields opened, San Francisco grew in population from about 800 people to nearly 35,000 people. A few years after that, the population reached nearly 255,000 people! San Francisco wasn't the only area experiencing amazing growth. It didn't take long for boomtowns to grow at crowded camps far off in the mountains.

Grass Valley, Nevada County, California.
(Photo courtesy of California State Library.)

THE GOLD CAMPS

*A*s miners arrived at gold sites, they built and lived in shoddy camps of tents and shacks. Soon some large camps began forming far off in the mountains at places where hundreds of miners lined up along streams and rivers panning for gold.

One such camp grew in western California at the southern end of the rugged Sierra Nevada Mountains. There, in the early years of the gold rush, a small group of prospectors set up a summer camp in a grassy valley. A small stream called Wolf Creek ran nearby. When cold weather came, the prospectors decided to round up their burros and leave. Then one of the miners found some gold-bearing rocks in the stream. Instead of leaving, the miners built a cabin and stayed through the winter. To miners passing through the valley, a cabin was a sure sign that gold might be nearby.

Within a short time, many miners arrived and spread out across the mountainous area. A few found rich deposits of gold. Several gold camps sprang up. Miners gave the camps names like Red Dog, Sailor's Flat, You Bet, and Gouge Eye. The town for the camps got its start on the grassy part of the valley and came to be called Grass Valley.

To supply the miners, a trader named A.B. Caldwell arrived and opened up his store in a battered tent. Having a source for supplies, the prospectors were able to pan for gold all winter, even though several severe snow storms struck the camp.

Even during the first year, the camp was bulging at the seams with nearly 10,000 people! The miners and merchants who stayed watched the town grow quickly as blocks of wooden stores appeared in the muddy streets. The boomtown of Grass Valley prospered. The town lasted many years as miners searched for every last bit of gold from the rich streams.

Grass Valley's most unusual resident turned out to be Lola Montez. She had made money working in dance halls in boomtowns. Eventually, she built a large house in Grass Valley and kept a number of strange pets that included animals such as monkeys, parrots, a grizzly bear and a brown bear.

James Wilson Marshall.
(Photo courtesy of California State Library.)

miners lived in makeshift and poorly built shelters. Most of the people there were men who worked long hours each day in icy stream water. One of Nevada City's more unusual residents was a woman miner. After she struck gold, she started a boarding house.

Within a short time the Nevada City prospectors picked out all of the surface gold from the stream beds and nearby land. A few prospectors started finding gold by digging shallow holes in the ground. Soon many prospectors were doing the same thing. These holes reminded people of coyote holes and the areas soon became known as "Coyoteville." As miners continued to find gold in this manner, Coyoteville continued to grow and prosper. Like other boomtowns, it consisted of many crude shacks and wooden buildings.

Eventually, the boomtowns of Grass Valley and Nevada City became almost twin towns. Merchants continued to open businesses as the populations grew. Mining in these towns went from prospectors working in the streams to miners actually digging their way underground to get at the gold beneath the surface. This kind of deep-shaft mining kept the towns alive in the early 1900s.

Around the time that Grass Valley was growing, other boomtowns were starting to appear in the mountains of western California. One of these was called Nevada City. Remember James Marshall, the same sawmill worker who had found the original gold that started the gold rush into the Territory of California in 1849? Well, Marshall had been digging at a place call Deer Creek when he found traces of gold. As usual, the news of the gold strike did not remain secret for long. Soon hundreds of other miners started arriving. When space for mining at the original strike disappeared, the miners spread out. Within two years the area had 10,000 miners.

The boomtown that served these miners was called Nevada, which is an Indian word for "snowy." However, when the state of Nevada joined the Union, the government officials said the boomtown had to change its name. After that it was called Nevada City.

Nevada City was like any other boomtown at first. Living conditions were miserable and many

ROCKY MOUNTAIN BOOMTOWNS

While the California boomtowns were growing, miners spread across the west seeking to make their fortunes in gold. The thirst for gold took miners into every possible place where gold might be found. Some miners in what was to become the state of Nevada, found enough gold and silver to make them rich. Prospectors in the southern part of the Rocky Mountains searched every stream and gulch they could find. Small strikes were made here and there. A gold rush almost as big as the one to California was about to start.

Hopeful miners heading for Colorado.

In 1858, some miners struck gold in the southern Rockies in the shadow of Pike's Peak near a place called Cherry Creek. Once again, the word got out that anyone could get rich simply by scraping the gold off the top of the ground. The Rocky Mountains were easier to get to than San Francisco had been in 1849. From states such as Missouri, the trip to the Rockies took only two or three weeks for those who traveled fast. The phrase "Pike's Peak or Bust" was on every gold seekers' mind and even painted on the sides of the wagons heading west.

Newspapers in the east told stories about the riches to be found near Pike's Peak and printed maps and directions for traveling there. People who left for Colorado traveled on horseback, in wagons, and in stagecoaches. Some people even walked. By 1859, nearly 50,000 had arrived in Colorado. Thousands of other hopefuls were still on their way or planning to head west.

The gold seekers formed a growing boomtown that was called Denver City. Easily accessible gold was cleaned from the streams and gullies in short order. There was still plenty of gold but it was inside minerals that were located deep in the ground. The minerals had to be mined and crushed, which required a great deal of money, machinery, and workers. Realizing that this was more work than they bargained for, many gold hunters turned around and went back home. Others decided to spread out from Denver and seek gold where the pickings were easier.

Many famous boomtowns grew in Colorado's Rocky Mountains as a result of these adventurous prospectors. While the miners searched for gold, they found other valuable minerals such as silver and lead. Even the cold winter months did not dampen the true believers' enthusiasm.

THE SILVER BOOMTOWN

*I*n 1877, a small tent and shack settlement started to grow in Colorado at a place called Leadville. It was located high in the mountains more than 10,000 feet above sea level. Miners had found silver there. Thousands of people arrived to cash in on the riches. To their dismay, miners in the early mountain boomtown found frozen ground and deep snow that covered the mountain until late spring.

For the earliest prospectors, life in the mountains was very harsh. In the winter, they often tunneled through ten feet of snow to find gravel to mine. Their first cabins were log huts made of small branches and earth for a roof. It was said that when people died in the winter, their graves had to be dug by blasting holes in the ground with dynamite.

Horace Tabor.
(Photo courtesy of Colorado Historical Society.)

One of the newcomers to Leadville was Horace Tabor. Tabor arrived in Leadville in the early 1860s. His wife, Augusta, was the first woman in the rough mining camp. The miners were not used to seeing a woman living in such miserable conditions. In a neighborly fashion, they set about building a small cabin for Tabor and his wife.

The Tabors remained in the booming town where he eventually opened a mining supply and grocery business. One day a miner with no money arrived in town. Tabor agreed to give him a large box of groceries for a one-third interest in any money the miner made on gold. In a few weeks the miner and a partner struck a rich vein of silver and Tabor became one-third owner of a flourishing mine. Eventually the mine was earning its owners about $250,000 a month!

Rich gold and silver strikes like that were the bait that drew thousands of miners to the Rockies. As towns like Leadville grew, unusual problems arose. High in the Rockies the climate was cold, and the only sources of heat were wood stoves and fireplaces. At one time nearly 2,000 lumberjacks were employed just to cut down trees. Firewood was used to heat Leadville's restaurants, hotels, gambling halls, and cabins.

It cost a lot of money to live in Leadville in those busy times. Everything for the town had to be brought in by large wagons pulled by teams of horses or mules. As the town grew, so did the number of wagonloads of supplies that arrived. Wagons carried merchandise such as clothing, food, mining equipment, mirrors, and whiskey for the miners and townspeople. Wagon trails up and across the mountains were steep and dangerous. Many a wagonload of merchandise slid off the trails and tumbled into the deep gulches. In the high mountains, the air has less oxygen. The horses and mules pulling the heavy loads up steep trails became winded quickly. Drivers had to stop and rest their teams every hundred yards or so.

As the town grew and prospered, many people went to work for large mining companies that had taken over the mines surrounding the town. The workers lived in town and worked deep in the mines. Others worked on the surface of the ground in buildings called "smelters." In smelters, workers extracted gold and silver from the rocks dug in the mines. In Leadville's busiest times, about 15 large smelters were located around the town. The smelly, noisy smelters added little pleasantness to the booming town of Leadville.

At this point in its growth, Leadville would not have been recognized by the original prospectors in the area. For a short time in its booming life, Leadville had the second largest population of any city in Colorado. In 1877, Leadville had under 250 residents. Three years later, after the boom, it boasted a population of 15,000. Fancy saloons, restaurants, and even a small opera house were built.

As Leadville was growing, so were other boomtowns in Colorado. One of them was called Cripple Creek. It is said that some settlers were working near a small stream when one of them shot off a gun by mistake. The noise scared a calf which tried to jump over the stream and broke its leg. The name of the stream stuck and later Cripple Creek became the site of a rich gold strike.

An old prospector found gold in a field that he used for a pasture. Few people would believe him at first because they said he drank too much whiskey and was always bragging about how he would find gold someday. Once the word got out that the strike was for real, miners and boomtowners arrived by the hundreds. Cripple Creek grew a little bit easier than most boomtowns because the streets and land for buildings were planned by the owner of the land. However, plenty of wooden buildings and shacks of all kinds stood as reminders of the very early days of the town.

In a short time there were businesses, rooming houses, some schools, and plenty of saloons. One day, two people who were having an argument started a fire. It quickly burned down a small part of Cripple Creek. A short time later, a fire much worse than the first destroyed most of the town. Hundreds were left homeless. When people in surrounding areas heard about the fire and hardship, they sent blankets, food, and clothing to help out. In those hard times, people pulled together and helped each other out.

At the height of the rush, the streets were alive with burros. Their braying kept the honest citizens of Leadville awake all night. (Photo courtesy of Colorado Historical Society.)

Another small boomtown in Colorado was called Kokomo. Like Cripple Creek, Kokomo was located high in the Rocky Mountains. The first prospectors to the area built their cabins on top of deep snow. Later, when miners struck rich veins of ore, workers carved steep, winding wagon roads out of the mountain sides. Boomtowns could grow only if there were roads to bring in supplies.

Dangerous roads were common in the mountains. Many a wagon driver told hair-raising tales of how he had to jump for his life as his wagon slipped off the road. Avalanches thundering down the mountainsides were another nightmare. These dangerous slides often swept away wagons, teams, drivers, and sometimes part of the road. In one town, people told the tale of a mail carrier whose wagon was hurled off the trail by a snowslide. Following that slide, winter storms piled drifts so high that the townsfolk were afraid to attempt a rescue. The wagon and driver were not found until the spring thaw.

THE COMSTOCK LODE

*O*ne of the most important boomtowns in the later years of the gold rush was established in the part of western Nevada called the Washoe. It was from there that an excited miner hiked many miles to a California town to have someone check the ore that he had found. The ore was rich not only in gold, but in silver. The strike became known as the Comstock Lode.

This rich discovery set into motion yet another stampede of desperate miners who wanted to get to the fortunes at the Washoe. Miners from eastern states as well as from California crowded onto trains, steamboats, or stage coaches heading for Nevada. Some miners had to wait weeks for space because all means of transportation had been sold out. To get to the Washoe area, miners had to travel the narrow, steep roads over the Sierra Mountains either on foot or in wagons.

Traders, realizing that a huge boomtown was in the making, offered fortunes to wagon owners to take supplies to the area. Soon, long stretches of the trail were clogged with slow moving teams of horses pulling heavy loads. One story goes that if a driver pulled off the trail for a time, he might have to wait hours for someone to let him back into line again.

Traveling with these miners and wagoneers was an assortment of people that made their money living off the miners—traders, merchants, gamblers, thieves, dance hall girls, blacksmiths, and about every other kind of worker of the time. At first they lived in tents or shacks. Many slept rolled up in blankets on the hillsides. The lucky ones slept in wagons, in crude shelters made of canvas, or in caves dug out of hillsides. Later, when cold weather arrived, temperatures dropped below freezing. Smoke filled the makeshift town as fires burned for warmth or for cooking.

Hundreds of people were arriving at the booming town each day. In honor of an old miner from Virginia, the town came to be called Virginia City. As people dug cellars or holes to support their cabins, they sometimes struck rock bearing silver ore.

As Virginia City boomed and flourished, bigger and finer buildings were erected. Many people got rich buying and selling their interests in the mines nearby. Some of the finest mirrors, wood, and cloth to ever reach a boomtown came across the mountains from San Francisco.

The rich supply of silver in and around Virginia City was important to the United States because it helped provide the money the North needed to fight the Civil War (1861-1865). Also, it helped make some men multimillionaires. These men would later invest their money in companies that built the railroads that would eventually connect the eastern states to the western states.

As these boomtowns were growing because of the rich strikes of gold and silver, some other kinds of boomtowns were beginning to spring up in the new state of Kansas.

A typical western boomtown street scene.

(Photo courtesy of Kansas State Historical Society.)

CATTLE BOOMTOWNS

Following the Civil War, the railroad builders extended their tracks westward. In the last half of the 1860s railroad tracks connected St. Louis, Missouri with Abilene, Kansas. Railroad trains were busy carrying all kinds of freight from eastern cities to western towns. However, there was little that the trains were taking eastward. Railroaders knew that empty trains did not earn money.

In the east, the population was growing. People needed fresh meat. During the Civil War years, Texas cattle had grown to number in the hundreds of thousands. Many were wild steers that roamed freely throughout the range. The nearest big market to take the cattle to be sold was hundreds of miles away. Few cattle were sold because of the distance required to move them.

Then, a businessman named Joseph McCoy had an idea. He figured out that the Texas ranchers could drive the cattle north to the railroad in Kansas. There, the cattle would be loaded on trains and shipped east to markets. In that way the ranchers would get their steers to market and the railroads would be full both ways.

McCoy went to Abilene, Kansas and arranged to have large holding pens built beside the railroad tracks. He also had ramps built so workers could drive the cattle from the pens directly into waiting cattle cars.

In the late 1860s Abilene was only a little frontier town with a dozen or so cabins and a trading post. The main street was dirty and dusty. After a rainfall, the street was full of puddles and thick mud. McCoy had a small hotel built to accommodate cattle buyers. Several traders and shopkeepers saw the opportunity ahead and set up their businesses to be ready for the cowboys bringing in the herds.

The cowboys would spend up to six weeks and sometimes more on the trail driving their herds northward. Herds ranged in size from a few hundred head of cattle to several thousand head. On the cattle trails, cowboys faced many hardships and dangers. There were swift rivers to cross and unfriendly Indian tribes to fight. Trails were dusty and the storms were fierce. Just about anything might spook the herd into a dangerous stampede. To get their herds safely to the railroad, the courageous cowboys had to overcome many hardships.

Cattle drives usually arrived in Abilene in the summer and early fall. During the first season, 35,000 steers arrived in Abilene to be shipped out on the railroad. Hundreds of cowboys, who were willing to spend a lot of money for a good time, accompanied the steers. Seeing money to be made, Abilene's businessmen and townspeople started preparing for the bigger cattle drives that were expected during future years.

Within three years, nearly 700,000 steers arrived in Abilene! Cowboys and ranchers who had brought the herds spent many thousands of dollars in lodging, food, supplies, and entertainment. Abilene spread out into a sizeable town. Business and professional people arrived. The town needed some law and order so officials hired judges and sheriffs. Settlers arrived to buy land for farms. Blacksmiths, barbers, gunsmiths, saddle makers, and other tradesmen opened shops. Families settled outside of town on small farms because the nearby stores offered places to trade or buy goods. Farmers started raising crops, meat, and foods to sell in town. Soon Abilene was not only busy during the summer and fall, when the cattle arrived, but all year long.

Left, cattle carts ready for loading.
(Photo courtesy of Kansas State Historical Society.)

When herds of cattle finally trudged into Abilene, cowboys received their pay and they were ready to celebrate before heading back to Texas. After spending weeks on the cattle drive the tiny town looked like the end of the rainbow to them.

Abilene stayed open most of the time so the cowboys could have fun all night. Piano music could be heard in the streets and kerosene lamps burned brightly inside the buildings. Lonely cowboys ventured into saloons where they could drink, gamble, and let off steam. There the hardships of the dusty trail were forgotten.

It was not unusual for a few cowboys to gamble away all of their money in a short time or spend it on whiskey. Still, many managed to buy clothes, boots, guns, bullets, and trinkets for people back home.

Occasionally cowboys ignored the boomtown's laws. They sometimes celebrated by galloping through town and shooting off their guns, sending honest citizens fleeing. Sometimes they got into arguments which were settled by gunfights.

Boomtowns drew unsavory gamblers who often cheated cowboys. They also had their share of thieves who roamed the dark streets at night looking to rob cowboys who had had too much to drink.

People who lived in Abilene soon tired of drunken cowboys shooting up the town. So officials passed laws to forbid cowboys from carrying their guns while in town. All weapons had to be dropped off at the sheriff's office. Separating a cowboy from his gun did not make for a happy cowboy. But that was just the beginning.

Soon the cowboys had a bigger problem. They were having difficulty getting their herds to the railroad near town. Trails into town were being blocked by barbed wire fences that farmers had erected to protect their fields. At first, the cowboys cut the barbed wire and drove their herds through the farmers' fields. This led to trouble and sometimes shootings. When enough farmers complained, town officials passed laws stating that no herds

Valley of the Teton
Public Library

could enter Abilene to be shipped by the railroad. Town officials wanted to rid themselves of the troublesome cowboys, saloons, and gambling houses. Herds would have to go elsewhere.

The town of Abilene had lived through its boomtown days and was becoming a quieter, settled place. Most of the people in town were glad the cowboys were gone. However, many of the businesspeople were disappointed. There was much less money in town. Cowboys no longer arrived to spend their money freely.

Cowboys had little trouble finding other places to take their herds. Several nearby towns were willing to put up with noise and outrageous behavior to get the cowboys' money.

The Dodge City Cowboy Band gave performances at the Long Branch Saloon.
(Photo courtesy of Kansas State Historical Society.)

DODGE CITY

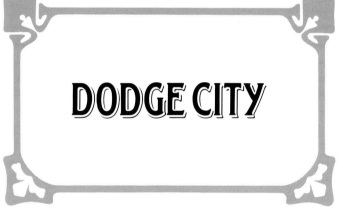

*D*uring the time that Abilene was booming, railroad builders were hard at work laying tracks farther west every day. The tracks had reached a small town in Kansas called Dodge City, 160 miles west of Abilene. At that time, Dodge City had one saloon and some traders near a frontier army post called Fort Dodge. The saloon was handy for the soldiers who went there to drink when they were not on duty. Buffalo hunters had been using it as a gathering place too. They had killed thousands of buffalo and had brought the hides and bones to Dodge City for shipment back east. In the east, people used the hides to make leather goods and ground the bones into fertilizer. As the buffalo became over-hunted and scarce, Dodge City needed something else to pump money into the town.

The few people in Dodge City were anxious and willing to take over the cattle shipping business that had been outlawed in Abilene. The small, dusty frontier town, sitting on the plains, did not have much else to offer newcomers.

The cattle business and cowboy money really brought Dodge City to life. Many of the owners of dance halls, gambling houses, and saloons in Abilene simply loaded their businesses onto wagons and moved them to Dodge. When they began moving in, Dodge had a population of only 1,200 people. All that changed quickly and soon twenty saloons and gambling houses opened to welcome the cowboys.

Dodge City shipped out its first trainload of steers in 1876. In a short time, large herds arrived. Some numbered nearly 5,000 head. At times, there were so many cowboys in town at once that the celebrating got out of hand.

Dodge City, like many other boomtowns, soon needed two cemeteries. One was for the towns-folk. The other was for lawbreakers and un-knowns who came to town, got shot, and died with their boots on. These men were buried —boots and all—in a special cemetery called Boot Hill.

The number of cowboys and gunmen who died with their boots on is often exaggerated. The exact number will never be known. Because of the wildness and shootings, officials in Dodge City did find it necessary to hire the best law officers they could find. These tough lawmen were pretty good at keeping peace and order.

Dodge had a few rules that helped keep things lawful. First, officials passed a town law stating that everyone had to leave his guns at the sheriff's office when he came to town. Second, the rowdy, noisy saloons that the cowboys liked to patronize had to move to one side of the railroad tracks. This made it easier for lawmen to watch for trouble. Third, town officials set up a system of charging lawbreakers large fines. That way, the boomtown collected plenty of funds and could afford to hire enough lawmen to keep order. In those booming days, frontier towns had some famous lawmen including Wyatt Earp, "Wild Bill" Hickok, and Bat Masterson. They all became well known in Dodge City's boomtown days.

Dodge's main street ran east and west to follow beside the railroad tracks. There were few shade trees on the plains in those days. The town was often hot and dry when the herds arrived. Still, Dodge was the greatest place on earth to cowboys who had spent dozens of nights sleeping on the open range and dozens of days eating dust in the saddle.

Living in town for a week or so after a long cattle drive was a special treat for cowboys who could afford it. A room and meals at a boarding house cost about $8.00 a week. For a bath, the cowboy usually went to the barber shop in town,

Edward Masterson accompanied his more famous brother, Bat, to Dodge City.

(Photo courtesy of Kansas State Historical Society.)

which had a back room with a large bathtub. A bath, which included hot water, soap, and a towel, usually cost about 25 to 50 cents.

In those days conditions on the frontier were not standing still. Things were changing rapidly. Other cattle towns were booming in the same way as Dodge. Kansas towns with names such as Ellsworth, Newton, and Wichita attracted cowboys and were wild, noisy places, just like Dodge City. Still, Dodge was considered the last of the cowboy boomtowns. The same railroads that carried the cattle out of Dodge and the other towns, were bringing in settlers and people who wanted to farm the land.

Farms started to appear outside of Dodge, as they did outside of Abilene, to choke off the cattle herds. The railroads had extended their rails far into Texas where herds could be loaded onto trains and shipped east. Ranchers no longer found it necessary to make the long, dangerous cattle drives. The booming growth of the cattle towns slowed down.

Front Street was the main street in Dodge City. The famous Long Branch Saloon is the second building on the left.

(Photo courtesy of Kansas State Historical Society.)

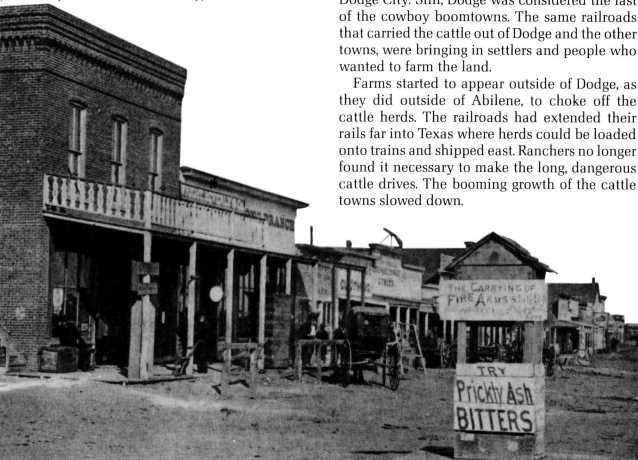

LIVING IN BOOMTOWNS

As more and more miners poured into the West in search of gold, mining camps and boomtowns spread out far and wide. In the early days of a boomtown, life was not easy. Men usually made up most of the population and they did not require many comforts. They were in town to make money or to celebrate.

Boomtown streets teemed with people and animals at all hours of the day and night.
(Photo courtesy of Colorado Historical Society.)

As a boomtown grew, its streets became packed with wagons pulled by teams of mules or horses. Many miners spent the coldest winter months in town rather than taking the chance of freezing in the mountains. Those who had arrived with burros often set them free. Many of the burros roamed through town day and night looking for food. At night the loud "hee-haw" braying carried through the thin cabin walls waking tired, sleeping residents.

Miners thought of boomtowns as temporary residences where they would remain only until they struck it rich and moved on. Because of this attitude, no one thought of establishing normal town services. Garbage was not collected; people threw it behind buildings. Rats feasted on the food that was thrown in the street. Miners usually didn't mind how the town looked—or smelled. To them, it was a place to have fun or to spend the winter when they could not work in the gold fields.

In the winter there were other worries. Blizzards and cold weather were dangers that could strike without warning. In the mountains, people had to watch for avalanches. In the spring when the snow melted, homes and cabins built too near streams or rivers often were washed away in raging floods.

Most of the town consisted of crude, unpainted, wooden buildings. At first, few were larger than an ordinary school classroom. They were often dirty and dusty, hot in the summer and cold in the winter. Fleas, flies, and mosquitos multiplied quickly and bit hard. Water had to be carried in buckets from town wells.

None of the buildings had indoor sinks or bathrooms. Townspeople had to use outdoor facilities called "outhouses." These outbuildings were built in the backyards of all the hotels, rooming houses, and cabins.

Electricity was not yet invented. Kerosene lamps or candles were used for light. News from the east often took days or weeks to reach the western towns. When enough people moved into a boomtown to settle permanently, someone began printing a local newspaper.

On the side streets, away from the shops and saloons, were the small shacks and cabins housing the people who worked in town. Farther outside of town were the cabins and barns of farmers who had settled nearby. The streets into and around town were usually full of ruts and animal droppings; not the most pleasant places to walk. Houses were close to the streets and

the dirt and animal droppings helped breed a multitude of flies and insects in the summertime. Because houses did not have screens on the doors or windows, it was impossible to get away from these little critters.

Small wooden shops were built along the main street. Most had roof-covered, wooden porches. The buildings were so close that the porches could be connected to make long, plank walkways which became the town's first sidewalks. Many shops had high false fronts to make them look bigger than they were. As the boomtown grew, newly opened stores stretched farther along the main street. Soon, stores in Dodge sold everything from boots to bullets. There were even livery stables where cowboys could get clean stalls, hay, and grain for their horses.

The general store carried everything from boots to bacon.